Perfect Disappearances

Perfect Disappearances

Poems by

Paul Hostovsky

© 2025 Paul Hostovsky. All rights reserved.
This material may not be reproduced in any form, published,
reprinted, recorded, performed, broadcast,
rewritten, or redistributed without
the explicit permission of Paul Hostovsky.
All such actions are strictly prohibited by law.

Cover image by Evelyn Goodstein

ISBN: 978-1-63980-792-5

Kelsay Books
502 South 1040 East, A-119
American Fork, Utah 84003
Kelsaybooks.com

for all the writers / writing

Acknowledgments

Thanks to the following magazines in which these poems and flash pieces, or earlier versions of them, first appeared:

10 By 10: "Over the River and Through the Woods," "Stealing Home," "Tassel of Wheat"
96th of October: "Coffee Run"
Acumen: "Passage"
BarBar: "A Modest Proposal"
Bluebird Word: "Beauty"
B O D Y: "Frieda," "Diminutive Wildernesses," "Baby Picture"
Caesura: "Picture of a House"
Chantarelle's Notebook: "Braille Lesson"
Clade Song: "Rethinking Rodentia"
Compressed Journal of Creative Arts: "Gift of the Acadians"
Feign: "Ergo Ego"
Harrow House: "Bazooka"
Hot Pot Magazine: "Little Puzzles"
I-70 Review: "*Conundra* Would Make a Beautiful Name for a Girl"
Last Stanza: "Death of the Pen"
MEARI: "Window"
Mid-Level Management Literary Magazine: "Grievance"
Midsummer Dream House: "What Happened with You Guys Anyway?"
Minyan: "Golden Rule Revised"
Naugatuck River Review: "Sunday Morning"
Off Course: "My Favorite Part of the Vacation," "O'Clock," "The Rub," "Thomas Lux, Poet Who Celebrated the Absurd, Dies at 70"
Only Poems: "Delve," "Flirting with the Deaf," "The Face of Listening," "Song"
Pineberry Literary Journal: "Grounded"
Please See Me: "Life Is Sacred"
Poets Online: "I Looked at Your Ass Because"

Prairie Home: "Money"
Sein und Werden: "Braille Trail"
Slant: "The Heart Is Hard to Find"
Thirteen Bridges Review: "Perfect Disappearances"
Wildscape Literary Journal: "Love Poem"
The Woven Tale: "Emu," "Luddite"
The Yesterday Review: "Goatscaping"

Contents

Braille Trail	15
Golden Rule Revised	16
The Heart Is Hard to Find	18
Frieda	20
Delve	22
Grounded	24
Diminutive Wildernesses	26
Baby Picture	28
Love Poem	30
Passage	31
Window	32
Tassel of Wheat	34
Rethinking Rodentia	36
Flirting with the Deaf	38
The Face of Listening	39
Sunday Morning	40
Emu	42
"Over the River and Through the Woods"	43
The Death of the Pen	44
Luddite	46
Money	48
Perfect Disappearances	49
Conundra Would Make a Beautiful Name for a Girl	50
Picture of a House	51
Gift of the Acadians	52
Little Puzzles	54
Goatscaping	56
Beauty	58
Thomas Lux, Poet Who Celebrated the Absurd, Dies at 70	60
A Modest Proposal	62
I Looked at Your Ass Because	63
What Happened with You Guys Anyway?	64
Song	66

Braille Lesson	67
Coffee Run	68
Grievance	69
Ergo Ego	70
Love Poem	71
The Rub	72
Hotel Ars Poetica	74
I Will Die in Florida	76
The Idiot	78
"Life Is Sacred"	80
O'Clock	81
My Favorite Part of the Vacation	82
Found Poem	83
Bazooka	84
Stealing Home	86

Braille Trail

I hid behind the blind guy—
a little in front, actually,
between a hand's breadth
and an arm's length,
offering my elbow. It was
the perfect disguise, no one guessed
it was the guy guiding the blind guy
through doors that opened clockwise
and doors that opened counterclockwise,
down stairs and over curbs,
through a turnstile into the carnival
where we ate our cotton candies
and threaded our way through the crowds
to the merry-go-round,
where I mounted a horse,
the blind guy a unicorn,
and we giddy-upped right out of there
while the calliope played.

Golden Rule Revised

I hate
the part of me
that hates.

It's only
a part of me—
apart

from that part
I am loving
and kind—

but still,
it permeates
the whole.

I have tried
loving
that part of me,

but that backfired—
if you love
to hate

you will hate wholly.
No, the only
way to restrain

the part of you
that hates
is to hate it.

You must hate
yourself
as you would hate others.

The Heart Is Hard to Find

When I got cancer I got a gun.
Because my father had cancer.
And he didn't have a gun.
And he didn't have a choice
but to let the doctors shake their heads
over the mutilated remnant
of his life—which they had mutilated
in their vain attempts to save it.
First they cut him open and took some things out,
and then they moved some other things around
so he had to shit in a bag after that.
This is no way to live, he said before he died.
He died when I was a kid,
and now that I have kids myself
I wonder: if my father had a gun
and if he had the balls—if one morning
when my mother was at work and I was at school
he got out of bed and in his gray bathrobe climbed
the little hill with the overgrown rock garden
that was our backyard
and sat down on a rock, just sat there
for a long time with the gun in his hand,
a long time being of course relative—
half a minute is an unbearably long time
when you're holding your hand over a flame—
thinking, perhaps, about me and my mother,
or perhaps just thinking about whether
to put the gun in his mouth or to his temple
or to his heart—because the heart would be less messy
but the heart is also hard to find—

feeling around for it with his left hand
on the left side of his chest, listening with his palm
for his own heartbeat, finding it,
then with his right hand
pointing the gun between the fingers
of his left hand over his heart,
taking aim like that and then
fucking doing it pulling the trigger killing himself
in his own backyard because
this is no way to live—
I am wondering now, if he had died like that,
would I ever have forgiven him?

Frieda

Nobody wants to hear a white guy going on about
all the Black people he has known, especially not
a white guy who hasn't known many Black people,
and especially not the first Black person he ever knew,
the live-in maid in his grandparents' house
whose name was Frieda, Frieda Farrell,
who did the laundry and the cooking and the cleaning
and the clearing, and served the food at his grandparents' table,
and came from Jamaica, and came from Newark,
and came when his grandparents called her
with a little silver handbell from Germany
that they kept on the dining room table next to their plates.

And nobody wants to hear him going on about
how Frieda would come when she was called,
walking slowly, limping a little (she was as old
as his grandparents, maybe older) into the dining room
from the kitchen where she ate her meals alone;
how the bell would ring and she'd put down her knife and fork
and enter the dining room in her uniform, a gray and blue
livery, and stand beside his grandmother or his grandfather
and wait until they spoke to her. And nobody wants to hear
how his grandparents kept a collection of those handbells
on a shelf above the sideboard, all of them silver and ornate,

or how he remembers picking one up and examining it,
admiring its heft, the craftsmanship of its carved wooden handle,
when suddenly Frieda came limping in from the kitchen
because he had called her. But he hadn't called her.
He hadn't meant to call her. He would never
call her or anyone with a little silver handbell. "Don't
play with that, it's not a toy," she had scolded,
then turned and limped back into the kitchen. Nobody wants to
    hear
how he can still hear that little handbell he never meant to ring,
how it goes on ringing in spite of what he means or doesn't mean.

Delve

I want to go deeper,
all the way down
to the cellar of the house
I grew up in. I go there
in my head, the same head
that easily cleared the low ceiling
above the dark, narrow staircase,
the lightswitch on the left,
the banister beginning halfway down
on the right, the aluminum nosing
of the treads groaning metallically
as I take the steps one at a time,
counting them as I go: one, two, three,
four, five, six, seven, eight—I think there were
ten altogether, though I could be overshooting it
or undershooting it. I can't
remember exactly but I can imagine
(imagination *is* memory) the exact feel
of the newel—small, rounded, wooden—
and the squeak-rub sound it makes
as I grasp it briefly like the hand
of a dance partner and twirl myself around it,
jumping off the last step with a flourish
and landing on the linoleum tiles
of the floor of the basement
of my childhood, the furnace room
(fire-breathing, verboten) on the left,
the laundry room (sweet-smelling, white)
on the right, and one central cylindrical
vertical pole silently supporting

everything above. I put my arms around it
lovingly, clamp my legs around it
tightly, and embrace it like a fire pole,
replacing my tight grip with a looser grip
to allow myself to descend.

Grounded

When I was little
and closer to the ground,
I spent a lot of time
on the floor. Sitting on the floor,
lying down on the floor,
crawling around on the floor
and playing with the cat
who was closer to the ground
than I was. I was
intimate with carpeting,
its smells, the soft scratch of its nap
on my cheek, the faint stains, fallen crumbs,
chair legs, table legs, heat registers,
a dead fly, dried husk of a bee,
corners, baseboards. The older
and farther away I've grown
from the ground, the more
I have forgotten the view
from down there. Now
I'm all up in my head all the time
and the only time I get down
on the floor is to look for the remote,
or to play with the kids. Grown-ups
mostly don't get down on the floor
if they can help it. But soon enough
we grow old, we fall down,
we have accidents, strokes,
heart attacks, and we find ourselves
suddenly on the floor again.

I hope when my time comes
I will remember to open my eyes to the infinite
ingredients of dust, endearing
dirt, scuffed shoe, imperfect
stitching of the welt, loveable
ankles of the living.

Diminutive Wildernesses

He was my best friend in 2nd grade
and 3rd grade and maybe 4th grade too. I don't remember
when it happened exactly, but he had a sledding accident
at the bottom of that hill we called Bunker Hill
in somebody's backyard, and I don't remember
why we called it Bunker Hill or who came up with that name,
and it may have been the other hill,
the adjacent hill, the one we called Devil's Pit,
and it's possible it wasn't even somebody's backyard
but one of those diminutive wildernesses
that grew between the backyards and the houses in my one and only
childhood. But he was my best friend
and then he had that accident and then
he was in the hospital for a long time because I think he broke his neck,
which was something people said, like *careful you don't break your neck,*
but I think he really did and I don't
remember visiting him in the hospital and I don't
remember what happened to him after that—
I think he may have gone to another school,
a school for kids in the hospital
or a school for handicapped kids, and I think I remember
seeing him once in one of those neck braces—
I think they call it a halo brace—it was screwed to his head,
but I could be imagining that because what I imagine
has completely overgrown what I remember,
the way a diminutive wilderness will overgrow
and swallow up a house where no one has lived for years.
Years later, I googled him and found him online.

He's an orthopedic surgeon now with a thriving practice
and gray hair and a neat beard in that photo of him on the hospital website.
And I emailed him through the website
and asked him if he remembered me.
I reminded him that we were best friends in the 2nd grade.
I asked him if he remembered what happened exactly,
how we had lost touch and wasn't it good to be in touch again?
But he didn't reply.
But I didn't give up because I had so many questions,
because we were best friends, so I emailed him again
and asked him about the sledding accident
and if it was what inspired him to become an orthopedic surgeon,
and he didn't reply again, and after a third email and no reply
I called the hospital and left a message for him.
I finally got a reply. It was short.
He said he preferred not to engage with me.
He used the word *engage*.
I was puzzled, angry, hurt.
I tried to remember what happened but I couldn't remember.
And now I think it's possible that maybe I abandoned him—
I mean after the accident I don't remember but I imagine
that maybe I didn't know how to be with him,
because he couldn't come out and play,
because he was in traction and he couldn't move,
because he had broken his neck,
which wasn't just something people said but something that happened to people,
and maybe that freaked me out and maybe I stopped
calling him, and maybe I stopped being his friend.
I really don't remember.
But I imagine he remembers.

Baby Picture

Of course I don't remember being that young—
nobody does. I don't remember

when I didn't know anything, when I thought
it was all about me, and my mother

didn't disabuse me of that thought,
which gave rise to other thoughts

about the world and everything in it,
thoughts I've been carrying around

in the world ever since I arrived
in the world. And now that I know

a thing or two, or think I know a thing or two,
I can't remember not knowing anything,

can't remember looking at my own hand as if
it weren't mine, putting it in my mouth—

putting everything in my mouth—to know it.
And how do I know a thing now?

How do any of us know anything now?
We spend our lives learning the world

by heart, putting everything in our hearts
and minds to know it. But we don't know it. Not

really. I think if I could only see my hand again
the way I did when I didn't know anything

I would suddenly understand everything.
I would put my hand up to my mouth the way

you do when you learn something shocking.

Love Poem

I love *I don't know*
because I don't
and neither do you
and neither does anyone

All these people saying
I think
and *I think that*
and *what I think is* . . .
I think I think I think—

What they should say is
I don't know
because they don't
and neither does anyone

But I know what you're thinking—
if you said *I don't know*
then no one would follow you
no one would listen to you
no one would quote you or vote for you
or love you

But I would love you
because I love *I don't know*
because I don't and neither
do you and neither does anyone

And if only if only
you would say *I don't know*
I don't know but I think
I could fall in love with you
forever

Passage

The book I'm reading now my mother read
and loved. You can get this close to the dead
and no closer. I like to imagine her smiling
or sighing over this passage, the marginalia
like lichen on a stone between the name and dates
and words from scripture. Her face is frozen now,
inanimate as the verdigris-covered headstones
in the cemetery I never visit because she isn't
there. She's here, in this book she loved—I can almost
see her gaze on the page, a faint patina covering
everything. I wonder what she said about this book
when she got to the last sentence. And if there was anyone there
to listen. I wasn't. There. And I wasn't listening. Away
at college, I wasn't reading much either, though I was allegedly
majoring in English literature. Mostly I was drinking
and smoking and making love or trying to, and feeling
motherless and existential. When she called I talked little, half
listening, scribbling on the wall beside the payphone.

Window

The doctor said what I have is called
pericarditis—inflammation of the pericardium,
which is the lining of your heart.

"We can cut a small hole—it's called
a pericardial window—to drain the fluid
around your heart and lungs. It's heart surgery

but in the world of heart surgeries
it's only a minor operation." It didn't
feel minor. The drainage tube hurt

like a motherfucker. I was in the hospital
for ten days and during that time I had plenty of time
to think about what it means to have

a window in your heart. The doc was less interested
in the figurative than the literal. He gave me
an incentive spirometer to take home.

An incentive spirometer is a device for improving
lung function. You're supposed to breathe into it
slowly and deeply. It looks like a cross between a bong

and a musical instrument. I already wore
my heart on my sleeve and now I was walking
through the world with a window in my heart.

I had a glass bong when I was a teenager,
back when I was in love with Faith Roffman,
the first one to whom I gave my heart.

She broke up with me for Mark Winkles
who could play lots of musical instruments
including the saxophone. That hurt like

a motherfucker and it felt like I couldn't breathe
as I walked around with a hole in my heart
for weeks, months. I got high all the time after that

and turned into a real pothead. I tried quitting—
swore it off by throwing the glass bong on the ground
which broke into a million pieces—but the next day

I bought another bag of weed. All these years later
in my convalescence, sucking on my incentive spirometer,
I'm thinking about Faith. I want to tell her

about the window, how it's possible to look
back and have these fond memories of the pain,
to smile warmly at the suffering. I want to tell her

about the strange alchemy
that turned my first broken heart at sixteen
into this cherished thing I caress like a polished stone

in a pocket, taking it out often, looking it over
fondly, turning and turning it
in the light of today.

Tassel of Wheat

That art teacher back in 7th grade, what was his name, Mr. Pessolano, I was thinking about him recently because I had the radio on and that Hall & Oates song "Sara Smile" came on, which is a great song, and I was singing along with it and then I was remembering this girl named Sara who was in my art class with Mr. Pessolano in the 7th grade, or maybe she was in 8th grade because I think she was a year or two older than me, but this was in junior high back when it was called junior high and 7th, 8th, and 9th graders were together in one school and Sara—I can't remember her last name—was pretty and a little goofy and she could draw Goofy as good as Disney and she never wore a bra, unlike the other older girls, and she was a really good artist, I mean she was talented, I mean she could draw people and animals and cars in this cartoon character way that was really impressive and I wondered whatever happened to her and then I remembered this pen-and-ink drawing I did in that class—it took me weeks, months—of a tassel of wheat, very detailed, all the florets, like hundreds of them on a single tassel of wheat and Mr. Pessalano said to take my time and draw each one, give each floret its own time and attention with that pen he let me use, which was a special kind of pen, a pen-and-ink pen, and I did exactly as he said and it turned out pretty damn good if I did say so myself—a tassel of wheat contains pollen grains which are the male genetic material that fertilizes the ovary of a kernel and we learned about that in science class that same year, all about anthers and ovaries and I knew enough to know that Sara had ovaries and of course she had breasts that you could almost kind of see behind the cloth of her stretchy shirts because she never wore a bra and I couldn't look at them and I couldn't stop looking at them and then I was thinking you know I may still have it somewhere in an old box in the garage, that drawing I did in the 7th grade, which was pretty damn good, hell it was great, and then I was thinking how all children are great artists, how I was a great artist myself once and how sad it is to grow up and grow out of greatness and I wondered if Sara was making a living somewhere maybe as a cartoonist, because she was great, and I tried googling her but without a last name the key words Sara, great, cartoonist, goofy, Millburn Junior High, braless didn't bring anything up.

Rethinking Rodentia

He pulls up in his pickup,
the names of rodents written
in an elegant cursive
that scrolls across the driver's door and around
the tailgate to the passenger side—*squirrels, mice, rats,
raccoons, woodchucks, moles, voles,
beavers, gophers, opossums*—
enumerating his catalog of services
the way contractors do their *retaining walls, patios,
porches, decks, roofs, siding, masonry.* This man
specializes in Rodentia. I found him
under Squirrels. I have squirrels under
my roof, squirrels in my walls, squirrels
in my sleep. "The largest rodent in the world
is the capybara," he whispers to me
as we stand together gazing up
at the suddenly conspicuous silence
emanating from my ceiling joists.
(They seem to know he's here.)
"It's a hamster the size of a sheep
or a sow. There's a family of them
at Southwick Zoo, across from the kangaroos,
catty-corner from the Patagonian
cavies. I visit them when I can." His plan
is to figure out where they got in,
set his humane traps, catch them one by one,
then plug the hole and drive a hundred miles west
to the Berkshires. "Any closer than that
and they'd find their way back." I like this guy
with his ladders and cages, his mercy and rodent
trivia: "*Rodens* is Latin for gnaw. They all
gnaw because they all have two incisors

that never stop growing. And gnawing
is the only way to keep them short. So you can't
blame them." I don't blame them. I thank him.
I pay him. And part of me wants to go with him,
ride shotgun out to the Berkshires,
keep listening, learning, rethinking
Rodentia, a large family of gray squirrels
barking and chirping in the cargo bed,
the names of rodents encircling us.

Flirting with the Deaf

I've been watching you watching the
interpreter. She is just to the left of the
speaker, and always slightly behind
so that you are always slightly behind
too, your face registering surprise
when the surprise has already been,
your smile on the heels of the other smiles,
your laugh coming after the wave of
laughter subsides. I love the lag time, the
pause between word and sign, the space
between signifier and signifier and
signifed. I want to slip inside that space and sit
across from you, legs crossed, hands
folded in my lap. If I made myself very
small, inconspicuous, insignificant as
another pair of antennae on the wall,
just watching you, quietly, watching the
interpreter, could I, could we, fit?

The Face of Listening

The active listening of Deaf people
in their signed conversations
with each other, if you've ever
seen them—beautiful, flitting,
leaping—communication as communion,
the almost-genuflecting heads
nodding their affirmations,
their agreements, their understandings,
the backchanneling, the feedback,
the empathic finger-flicked HOW-AWFUL,
the bobbing OH-I-SEE,
incredulous TRUE-BIZ?
in-the-face WOW! the approving
and allowing and concurring
RIGHT-RIGHT and YES-YES
and THAT-THAT-THAT—
all that grammar of the face, its tenses,
its *anima*, the thousand outpouring faces
of Deaf people listening to each other's
gab, palaver, repartee, the found
poems, the stories, jokes and autobiographies
in a language with its own music—
rhythms, assonances, crescendos
and descrescendos, riffs and repetitions—
all the sections of the body's orchestra—
hands, face, eyebrows, eye-gaze,
lips, tongue, head-tilt, shoulder-turn—
creating meaning simultaneously—voilà—
a visual-gestural symphony for the eyes.

Sunday Morning

It was a mostly Jewish neighborhood
but up on Main Street there was a church
with a sign out front: *Jesus Saves.*
I had heard of Jesus and I was saving
for a new bicycle myself,
so I leaned my old bicycle against a tree
and climbed the front steps
and tried the front door. It was unlocked, unlike
the Essex Savings Bank across the street
where I had an account with $32 in it.
I stood there on the threshold, hesitating,
until I heard someone say, "You are welcome."
So I said, "Thank you,"
which was the first backwards thing
among a whole host
of backwards things I saw and heard
as I tiptoed in and took a seat in the last row,
which was the first row if everyone
turned around and faced the sunny
summer Sunday outside.
But they were all facing the darkness up front.
And when my eyes adjusted I saw angels
on the walls and ceiling,
and people standing and people kneeling,
and people waiting in line to go up front
where a man in a white robe deposited
something into their mouths.
Then they made these signs on their heads and chests
not unlike the third-base coach in baseball,

and pretty soon someone was tapping my shoulder
because it was my turn now
to go up there for the deposit.
And that's when I ran outside and down the steps
and started pedaling as fast as I could
back into the sun.

Emu

I dreamed you the emu at the zoo.
The sign said you bit, but you blinked
so sadly. You had

no hands. You looked
flabbergasted to be there.
Speechless for the first time in your life.

You could only cock your head in that birdlike way
and bite the wire mesh with your beak, but I knew
the word you were trying to say

was *mistake*. Your favorite word
in the whole world. But there was no mistake.
After all, this was *my* dream. I was having it,

and I wasn't having any of your
biting, supercilious,
inventory-taking editorial

in my dream, I said
in my dream. Then I moved on
with my fistful of corn

to the fallow deer
who are always more timid
than hungry.

"Over the River and Through the Woods"

Drove all the way out to my grandmother's house in South Orange the other day, after some business in Brooklyn, just to have a peek—she'd been dead for thirty years and I'd been living up in Boston for longer than that—and though the house looked pretty much the same as I remembered it, there was now a sign out front that said St. Paul's Catholic Outreach. Something possessed me. I walked up the long driveway and rang the bell. A young novice answered the door and I told him my grandmother used to live in this house, that I remembered coming here for Shabbat dinners when I was a kid, and would he mind if I had a look around? He was very gracious about it and introduced me to the priests and other novices who lived and prayed in the house together and helped each other with things like "discernment." Which I misheard as "the sermon." "You help each other with the sermon?" I asked him. And he said, "No, with discernment." And I said I knew the word but wasn't sure how he was using it. And he said it meant helping each other to discern the voice of God as opposed to your own wistful, wishful thinking. And I didn't know what to say to that, so I said, "Hey look, the mezuzahs are still here in the doorways where my grandfather installed them," which wasn't a total non sequitur. And then they gave me the tour of the house which basically still looked the same as it did all those years ago because they hadn't done any renovations, maybe because the Church couldn't afford it, or maybe because of the vow of poverty and all that. The bathroom still had the same pink and green tile that I guess was in fashion back in the 1960s. It was a real blast from the past to walk through that old house where I hadn't set foot since I was a kid, and in the front hallway, where there used to be a large ornamental mirror with a gilded frame that me and my cousins used to pull faces in, there was now a simple, unadorned wooden cross. But I was pretty sure I could discern the shadow of that big old mirror, the shape of it, like a picture-frame shadow that's left on the wall after the picture has been removed.

The Death of the Pen

Everybody's got a device.
But here is this guy
asking if anybody's got a pen—

I have a pen.
Because I always have a pen.
Because I'm always writing

and I'm always reading
and I'm sitting here now with this book,
turning the pages,

a pen in my shirt pocket,
a poem in progress folded in half,
then folded in half again

and again—an origami bird
that flits and fits
on an eighth of the page

in my pocket. I am reluctant
to volunteer my pen to this guy.
Because everybody has a device

and I don't like devices and I don't like
movies based on books
that people with devices watch on their devices.

He has noticed the pen in my pocket.
He is asking if he can borrow it.
I lie to him: It just ran out of ink, sorry.

That's okay, he says, he only needs it
to insert into the reset hole of his device
so he can finish watching the movie.

Checkmate. I give up
my pen. Soon he hands it back to me
with a thank-you and triumphant smile.

I gaze down at the pen where it lies
horizontal in my palm, unburied
fallen soldier I was married to.

Luddite

Part of me, a very big part, like 98%, wants to toss this laptop
into the garbage can (which I really shouldn't do because
it would end up in a landfill and leak rare earth elements)
and write this poem instead with a pen or pencil on a piece of
    paper.

And that same part of me, which is greater than the sum of the
    other parts,
wants to jettison the television, the smartphone, and the car,
in that order (because I'll need the car to take the television and the
    laptop
to the recycling center, and the phone to pay the cathode ray tube
    recycling fee

with my recycling app). That's the side of me—the side that I am
    on—
that is against airplanes, cruise ships, credit cards, online banking,
    video games,
social media, free shipping, and plastic. All plastic. Especially the
    plastic
that protects our food and prevents waste. And especially the
    plastic

that's used in hospitals to save our lives: disposable syringes,
    surgical gloves,
blood bags, IV tubes, catheters, plastic heart valves. Because
    what's the point
of saving our lives when the plastic is killing us? Or of protecting
    our food
with plastic when the plastic is in our food, and in our water, and in
    our air,

and in our poetry—just look at all the plastic in this poem! And I
    wasn't even
thinking of writing about plastic. But here it is. It's everywhere!
    And a big part of me
wants to toss this poem because of all the plastic in it. But a small
    part, like maybe
2 parts per million, kind of likes this poem and wants to put it out
    there in the world.

Money

"I'm paying with cash," he says.
"Real money. Not plastic. Not
numbers in a cloud. Real smackers
that you can hold in your hand
and smell. Like in the old days.
I miss the old days." And he smacks
the crisp twenty in his hand,
sniffs it, lays it on the counter
and smooths it with both hands.

She waits three beats, picks it up
and puts it in the register, tap-tapping
a roll of quarters against the drawer,
the real money spilling out in a clinking
cascade. She counts out his change,
presses it in his palm. "Hell," she says,
"if you miss the old days, why not pay
with cowrie shells. Or better yet, a camel
or a cow. Livestock was the first money.
And it smelled like money."

Perfect Disappearances

This poem is for all the writers
writing. On their laptops, desktops, smartphones,
legal pads, napkins, palms
of their hands—desperate to get it down
before it disappears
like the phone number of the most amazing person you just met
and have to see again—just have to—
so you write it on your own skin
and walk off into the world alone
with the whole world in your hand. God
help the writers in love with the words that disappear
like disappearing trains you catch
by running after them,
losing a shoe, a hat, an earring, a spouse—a lifetime
of chasing the disappearing words,
breathlessly reaching for them,
grabbing ahold and hoisting yourself up
onto the caboose, entering the rhythm
of those corridors moving through the world
as you move through them, feeling your way,
looking up and down and all around for
that dream you dreamed and followed all the way here.

Conundra Would Make a Beautiful Name for a Girl

In the dream we had birds
in the house, so we had to open
all the windows to let them out
which was how they got in
in the first place, which was
the conundrum in the dream.
One alighted on the newell
at the bottom of the staircase
so I grabbed it gently but
firmly—a bird in the hand in
the dream—I didn't want to hurt it
but I didn't want it to get away,
which was another conundrum
in the dream. Outside I set it down
on a picnic table that sprouted up
in the dream, but it didn't fly away—
it just lay there the way you lie
on your side when you're sick
or on your back when you've hurt
your back. I worried I had hurt it
even though I'd meant to free it,
and I wondered what it meant,
this dream about birds in the house
with a bird in the hand I hadn't
meant to hurt but hurt anyway.
I wrote it all down in the dream
and wandered through the dream
looking for an interpreter of dreams
to tell me what it all meant.

Picture of a House

Your mother and father speak English with a foreign accent.
You don't have their foreign accent but you are made to feel
foreign because of them. You are from here but you are also
from them. So you are foreign by association. This embarrasses
    you
and you want to disassociate from the impossible-to-ever-fix-fully
broken English and its long, sad, hopeful, amazing story, which is
a success story. But to your ear it sounds like failure. Your friends,
when they come over, can't help laughing at the funhouse
    distortions
of the English, the ungainly vowels and consonants flap-flapping
in the air around your house. And pretty soon you stop inviting
your friends to your house. And pretty soon you're old enough
to leave home yourself. And you don't come back and you don't
look back. And your huge embarrassment shrinks and fits inside
the telephone with your parents, who also shrink. And you don't
let it out and you don't let them out. They live inside the tiny holes
of the telephone for years, saying they miss you and when are you
coming home? Eventually they die in there—they die inside the
    telephone
and it feels a little like you suffocated them. And then, finally,
when you do come home, the weeping hits you like an attack of
    dyspnea,
like all the windows in the house—all those little pieces of sky
that you used to breathe through just by looking out of them—
    looking out
and away—are covered now. Not the mirrors, but the windows
are covered. So you're forced to look inside. And see yourself.

Gift of the Acadians

He was the only Deaf person in his family. And he kept to himself mostly. Because no one in his family bothered to learn how to sign. He didn't learn it himself until they sent him away to the school for the Deaf, where he lived during the week. He only came home on the weekends. For years and years. And home began to feel less and less like home. Because the language of home wasn't his language. Because ASL was his language. So home was the school for the Deaf where everyone signed. And that's where he met his future Deaf wife. She took his last name, which was an old French name. A name that went all the way back to the French Acadians who fled Nova Scotia during *Le Grand Derangement* and settled in the American colonies. And the French Acadians kept to themselves mostly. Because the American colonists didn't speak French. So there was a lot of inbreeding—cousins marrying cousins—which must have been how a recessive genetic quirk got passed all the way down to the little Deaf boy. Who thought he was the only one. But he wasn't the only one. His wife was Deaf and pretty soon they had their first child, and that child was born Deaf. And he and his Deaf wife didn't know what to think. They laughed and rejoiced. And two years later, the twins were born Deaf. And they laughed and rejoiced again. And again. And home was ASL. And he and his Deaf wife and children were home. And he was never so happy in his life. A life in which he had thought he was the only one. But he wasn't the only one because the others were all on their way. And they'd been on their way all that time. They were a long time coming. But here they all were now. And he supported his growing Deaf family by working for the post office as a letter carrier. He delivered letters for over forty years. By the time he retired he was a grandfather. And his four grandchildren were Deaf. And their tiny flying hands and beautiful animated little faces were a gift. And this was the gift of the Acadians. This quirky, genetic gift. And it was a precious gift in spite of what the doctors and audiologists said. It was a hidden gift that took a long time to be found. But a short time to unwrap. The gift of a large Deaf family—Deaf children, Deaf grandchildren, Deaf sons- and daughters-in-law. All signing beautifully, elegantly, eloquently. All gathered around the old Deaf grandfather. Who was never so happy in his life.

Little Puzzles

They came with their heavy equipment at 7 in the morning.
A crane, a bucket truck, a transport truck with those iron
palings, two dump trucks and a chipper. The doomed trees,
each marked with a spray painted red bindi, stood quietly
with their eyes closed, swaying a little in the breeze,
looking perfectly calm, perfectly healthy, perfectly
innocent. I was having second thoughts as the men in work boots
descended on my lawn, smoking their cigarettes and yelling to
    each other
over the roar of the crane engine. I had agreed
on six thousand dollars for twelve massive pines. "You'll sleep
much easier knowing they're gone," said the guy who gave me
the estimate, pointing out the ones that threatened the house.
A smaller one had fallen last summer on the roof above my
    bedroom
during a windstorm. "You're lucky it wasn't one of these—
any of them could have killed you in your sleep," said this man
    who made his living
killing trees. There was a war going on out there—who knew? And
    yet the trees
looked so peaceful, so majestic, so condemned—the crane operator
carefully backing the mammoth machine into my tiny backyard,
    trampling
the roses. I didn't stay to watch the carnage. I left for work,
or what I call work—nothing so physical or strenuous or violent
as cutting down twelve 150-foot coniferous trees in the prime
of their lives. My work is smaller, safer, quieter. Words mostly—
considering them. Collecting them. Putting them together. My little
puzzles. When I got home the men were gone, the trees were gone,

a faint smell of pine in the air, huge divots in the grass where the
    crane
had been parked. And lots of little twigs and pine cones littering
    the lawn, sticky
with sap, left to me to pick up, to sniff, to consider, to put together.

Goatscaping

This morning I noticed two small green tomatoes
in the garden. I guess things are getting started
after all. Everything in its own time. And speaking
of nature having its way, have you heard of
goatscaping? I love the name, the play on words.
There's this guy in Dover who owns a natural landscaping
    company
called Goats of Dover—he'll bring his goats over
and clear your property of the unwanted weeds
and biomass the natural way, letting his goats
do all the work. They'll eat anything and everything.
I called for a free estimate because the weeds
and saplings and poison ivy—and especially
the black swallow-wort—have been encroaching on my house
like they're going to swallow it up. I want to cut them back,
get rid of the invasive species, maybe plant some wildflowers
or native vegetation that won't go haywire. So the guy
came over last Sunday with a measuring wheel
and a clipboard. He had a billy goat's beard and a ponytail
and smelled faintly of goat and looked vaguely like a goat
    himself—
you can't make this stuff up. He knew the names
of all the plants. And as he perused my property (I have
three-quarters of an acre) he taught me the names of what I have,
including the aforementioned black swallow-wort. And then
he said uh-oh, I see you've got some lily of the valley,
pointing at some ground cover that I was familiar with because
I have a ton of it. But I never knew the name of it. And I said
oh that stuff is everywhere. And he said that's going to be a
    problem—

lily of the valley is toxic to goats. They can eat just about anything
but there are a few species that make them sick, and some
can even be lethal. And lily of the valley is one. I showed him
where it grew on the other side of the house by the forsythia
and also among the saplings. He shook his head and sucked his
     teeth,
said sorry, it's a deal breaker—if it were only here and there
I could cordon it off with some electric fencing
to keep the goats from eating it. But considering
the extent of it, well, nice to meet you. And he climbed
back into his pickup. So much for goatscaping,
but I'm thinking I might try writing about it,
because although I'm not very good at writing about nature,
this guy with his goats, who put me in mind of a goat himself,
isn't he just begging to be made into a poem?

Beauty

The way her hands danced across the braille page, it was a beautiful choreography to behold. Her left hand beginning each line, handing it off to her right hand halfway across the page, the right hand finishing the line as the left moved down to begin reading the next line. Left hand to right hand to left hand to right hand. Expert, fleet, like a concert pianist, or like relay runners in a race, the handoff accomplished seamlessly over and over, line by line down the page, page by page through the book, book by book through his entire childhood.

There was never a time when he didn't know it. He'd learned it with his ABCs, fingering the raised dots with his tiny hands, sitting in his mother's lap as she read to him aloud from the print/braille children's books while he looked at the pictures. B was *but,* C was *can,* D was *do.* M was *more.* M with a dot in front was *mother.* White dots on a white page, but they cast these tiny shadows so he could see them in the light. Like a country of igloos as seen from an airplane on a sunny winter morning.

Having blind parents was as unremarkable as having breakfast in the kitchen, having mail in the mailbox, having rain on rainy days and sun in the summertime. Lending his mother or father his shoulder—his elbow as he grew taller—was like offering his arm to the sleeve of his own jacket, like giving his hand to his other hand. He thought nothing of it, didn't even have a word for it until he started kindergarten and the word got spat on the ground by some ugly mouths on the playground, older boys snickering and pointing, mimicking his parents as they swept their white canes back and forth, back and forth. *Click sweep, click sweep, click sweep.*

Those white canes. At home they leaned quietly against the wall like backslashes in the unpunctuated dark. Or else they sat folded underneath a chair or table like bundles of long chalk, a red one in each. K was *knowledge*. P was *people*. And the braille dictionary in seventy-two volumes was stacked practically to the ceiling, like a cord of wood.

His mother would stop reading, open her watch then close it, *click*, reach under her chair for her cane and open it, *chick-a-chick*, into a white line which she swept across an invisible line which she walked, out the door and down the street to the grocery store. Q was *quite*, U was *us*. Braille was dots in a cell, lots and lots of cells. Each cell was a three-story building at dusk, the lights on in certain windows, not others. Each book was a city, where he and his mother looked through the windows, their fingers pressed to the panes.

Outside it's beginning to snow. And each snowflake is a different character in the Complete Works of Beauty, which contains no mistakes that he has ever been able to find. And he has looked—he has spent a lifetime looking—but has never found a single mistake.

Thomas Lux, Poet Who Celebrated the Absurd, Dies at 70

—New York Times obituary

I don't think he would have appreciated that.
And I don't mean the dying, or even
the number—a nice round respectable number—
so much as the choice of the adjectival noun: *the absurd.*
Or is it a nominalized adjective? He would have
liked the question, the not quite knowing, or caring,
or saying one way or the other in the poem,
if it were his poem. Which I like to think it sort of is
now that he's dead and the writer of his obituary
got the headline wrong (like getting the headstone wrong)
and it's left to me to right it: Thomas Lux
celebrated *life* (which, OK, is, granted, sometimes, yes,
absurd). He celebrated *truth.* "I like the story because
it's true." And *beauty.* And *love.* Always love. Which is
"always, regardless, no exceptions . . . blessed." It's a missed
opportunity, he called it in his workshops, when we don't
call on the right words, the ones that are dying to be chosen,
as though sitting in a classroom with their hands raised
high, higher, practically levitating in their seats. *Absurd*
isn't the right word. He was funny, yes, but dead
serious about the poems. He had fine, caramel hair
as long as a girl's, but he had a mean lefty sidearm
that always hit home. He had lousy eye contact in front of the
    class,
or when standing up at the podium reading his poems,
but his gaze in the poems is laser, unflinching, lapidary.
Not a bad list, he would have said (three or more
adjectives make a list) but you can do better. Write
harder. This poetry business is hard work. "The thing
gets made, gets built, and you're the slave . . ."

He slaved over every word, every pause, every line break.
"You make the thing because you love the thing."
We love his poems because he loved them enough
to make us love them. *Absurd?* "Give me, please, a break!"

A Modest Proposal

Let's get rid of all the carnivores, why
don't we? It would go a long way toward
world peace. I mean do we really need
all those birds of prey? Wouldn't the common
house sparrow, which is able to perform
complex tasks like opening automatic doors
to enter a supermarket, be a more appropriate
national bird than the bald eagle? I mean
think about it: if we lost all the lions
and tigers and bears, the cats and dogs,
and the humans who can't make the switch
to vegetarianism, wouldn't life be kinder and
kind of sweeter? OK, maybe you're thinking
a world without dogs is no place you'd ever
want to live. And yes, though the sparrow's diet
consists mainly of seeds, it does eat the occasional
animal: beetles, caterpillars, flies and aphids,
among others. OK, I withdraw my nomination
of the sparrow for the national bird, but hear
me out: we'd still have elephants. In fact
we'd have way more elephants than we have now,
not to mention gorillas, rhinos, horses and cows.
And all those humans who wouldn't hurt a fly.

I Looked at Your Ass Because

the physiology of vision,
which is the process by which
human beings actually see,
says we see best at the center
of our cone of vision, the way
the focal point in a painting
pulls you in, drawing in the light
to your retinas where your photoreceptors—
all your rods and cones—are hard at work,
the rays of light meeting and reflecting
and refracting and diverging
and proceeding as you proceeded
radiantly past me down the street,
so it was more of a scientific observation
than a gawking—I wasn't gawking—
as I looked at your ass as your ass
moved in that way it has of moving
as you moved in that way you have
down the sidewalk, my scientific
observation focused on the slender body
of research concerning the question
of how a refulgent ass such as yours
is able to draw in all the light
of the universe.

What Happened with You Guys Anyway?

because what I heard was
you both walked away
from your unhappy marriages,
two children each,
to be with each other,
that it started at work
the way it sometimes does,
that you'd worked together
closely, the kind of closely
that can sometimes lead to play,
the kind of play that can
turn serious in a heartbeat, a head-tilt,
a glance then a glancing away,
then a looking back again,
a smile that turns suddenly hungry,
which I heard it did,
and it turned everyone against you
when they heard what you did,
leaving your families for each other—
but I want you to know
when I heard I was first of all
happy for you, and maybe also
a little titillated to think of you both
finding love among the cubicles,
right there on the desk or maybe
under it on the floor,
and when I heard the grumblings
and judgments and condemnations,
I felt compelled to send you
that Hallmark card, did you get it?
because *Congratulations*
seemed the right thing to say somehow,

but then more recently I heard
that you're not together anymore,
or rather, you're still working together
but you're not *together* together,
and I thought to myself that's gotta be hard,
and I know it's none of my business but
what happened with you guys anyway?

Song

Sex is weird, don't you
think? I mean take my nose
in your handkerchief. I mean
who doesn't want to rub up against
Beauty? Get a little of it on your
eyelids, in your nose, get inside its
dark, sweet, monogrammed folds
for a good sneeze? It's a little
weird, a little gross, but I would
kiss you where you pee if you would
let me. Bless me, don't you think it's
Fate? I mean you and me in Beauty's
corner? I mean me rooting for Beauty
in your lap? And don't you think
Whoever thought this up was
Weird? I mean what was She
thinking? Love is life licking itself
prolific. I think it's all just one big
Tongue. And I don't think it means
anything. And I think about it all the
time. I mean all the time. Don't you?

Braille Lesson

"Stop rubbing," says your braille teacher
because you keep rubbing the dots
up and down, up and down,
to feel them better. Because they're hard to feel.
And the tip of your finger feels so dull
that you wish you had a pencil sharpener
for your index. "Just let it glide slowly
across the page, softly but firmly,
and without rubbing." But the thing is
rubbing feels good, so you do it, and you keep on doing it,
which reminds you of other kinds of rubbing you have done.
"It's hard not to do it," you tell the teacher
whom you can't see but can feel nodding sympathetically.
Rubbing is the only way you can make sense
of the dots. There are six of them—
two columns of three—in every braille cell.
Each position has two possibilities: dot
or no dot. So what you're doing is essentially
a very soft whack-a-mole with the whorl of your index.
There are sixty-four possible combinations
of the six dots. Two to the sixth power, or two times two
times two times two times two times two.
You're a safe cracker trying to intuit
the combination by feel. "You're rubbing again,"
says the teacher. If only you could
break in, grab the gold, the treasure. Grasp it.

Coffee Run

"Hey Bob,"
I said to the nabob
sitting under the baobab
in the lotus position.

Bob was a kind of
nickname, a kind of
diminutive, a kind of
presumption, really, him being

a nabob and all.
Like Jesus, Buddha,
Muhammad et al.
he was rich in the spiritual
sense, but ever since

the recession of 2008
he was poor in the dollars-and-cents
sense. "Hey Bob, you got
50 cents? Let's consolidate
and get a cuppa joe."

He flinched as though
the proposition were a fly
alighting on his unibrow.

Then, slowly, mindfully,
he dipped a crimped hand
into his dhoti, extracted
a crinkled dollar bill

and offered it up to me
like a moist and crumpled prayer,
without opening his eyes.

Grievance

So I take my grievance to the grievance coordinator, but she doesn't really address it, I mean she basically writes me off, so then I have a grievance against the grievance coordinator, which is a more grievous grievance than the original grievance, which I won't go into now because it would only distract from the egregiousness of my grievance against the grievance coordinator, whose job it is to address the grievances of the aggrieved. So I ask her for the name of her supervisor because this is totally unacceptable and I want to go over her head and escalate my grievance, and her supervisor's name is Egon. So I write this Egon a long excoriating email concerning my grievance against the grievance coordinator and three weeks go by and I don't hear back from him. So now I have a grievance against the grievance coordinator's supervisor, and where am I supposed to go with this grievance? I mean where is this leading? I mean where will it end? I mean is this America or some badly translated Kafkaesque novel I'm living in? And then finally this Egon replies with a one-liner whose mangled syntax smacks of transliterated Czech or Russian or Bulgarian or I don't know what foreign language: "Do you not be happy with her as the coordinator of the grievance of you?" So now I have a grievance against the whole world for trying to learn English, the new lingua franca, and for tormenting me with its mutilation. And where in the world am I supposed to go with that grievance I'd like to know.

Ergo Ego

It came to him in the shower. Which was where he got all his best ideas. He was thinking about himself. Actually, he was thinking about other people thinking good things about him. Which always made him feel good. Happy even. Ego is a source of happiness, he thought to himself as he rinsed the conditioner out of his hair and stood a little longer under the jetting streams, considering the possibilities. Then he smiled to himself as he stepped out of the shower, the same self he couldn't quite see in the fogged-up mirror, which he wiped clean with a corner of the towel, then padded over to the laptop in the kitchen, his wet footprints evaporating as he searched for Ego on the baby-names website. Nothing between Egbert and Egon. Hmm. But he couldn't help noticing that December, January, and February—sources of happiness for people who love winter—were popular, non-gendered names. "What would it take," he asked his wife, the bulging bowl of her belly obliquely reflecting the salad bowl in which she was tossing their lunch, "for Ego to make the cut? Think self-esteem, self-worth, self-love, ergo a source of happiness, the kind of happiness you'd want to name a child after." She stopped tossing, gave him a withering look. It withered the lettuce, the lunch, the whole family tree, all the way down to the little blossom curled up inside her. "It would take what linguists call a semantic change," she said, "which could take a few hundred years. But not in a million years would I name a child of mine Ego. What is the matter with you? Are you out of your tree?" "OK," he said. "Forget it. It was just a thought." A not entirely unworthy one, he said to himself.

Love Poem

I don't like the way you read
and I don't mean
aloud. I mean you read too fast,
too facilely, too faithlessly.
I mean we both read that book
and loved it—you said you loved it—
but then you moved on to another book,
another voice, while I still had the voice
of that book in my head
and I couldn't move on. I went back
and lingered in the copyright history,
the blurbs, the epigraph and dedication,
then I reread the first sentence, the first
paragraph, the first page,
and it was like love at first sight a second time
as I dove back into the book we loved,
and I'm loving it still
and reading it again. Don't talk to me
about the book you're reading now.
Don't tell me you're loving that book.
You don't know what love is.

The Rub

"You like?"
She barely
spoke English.

"I like."
I met her my junior
year abroad—

Gauloises.
Baguettes.
Croque Monsieurs.

Art museums.
"You like?"
"I like."

I stopped
going to class,
hung out with her instead,

smoking and drinking
Beaujolais and Stella
Artois. I learned

some French
that wasn't in the book.
She gave me

her tongue.
I gave her mine.
I knew her

intimately
and not at all.
And that was

the tragedy:
To like or not to like
was the only

question.

Hotel Ars Poetica

The reader
is a guest here
and you're the manager
and the bellhop
and the maintenance man
and the boiler in the basement
needs a tune-up
and the doors that open clockwise
and the doors that open counterclockwise
need oiling
and everything needs polishing
and some things always need fixing
like the line breaks
even if they ain't
broke
period
and all punctuation
is optional because
we don't coddle our guests
we treat them with
you thought I was going to say
respect
didn't you
but the operative word is
intelligence
and another operative word is
and
and and and and
because this hotel has many rooms
and it employs
an additive syntax
and intelligence

and humor
and you're the night auditor
and the devastatingly handsome
pool boy
and the bellhop
and the maintenance man
so you better
start maintaining baby
and give the reader
a hand

I Will Die in Florida

which is the state with the prettiest name,
or so said Elizabeth Bishop
who died in Boston, Massachusetts,
or so said Mark Anderson from West Virginia
who had read more Bishop than I had
when I met him at that college on the Hudson
where we were English majors. *Venereal soil,*
said Wallace Stevens about Florida,
or so said Robert Kelly, our professor and resident poet
who weighed over 400 pounds. I didn't care for Stevens
and I didn't care for Kelly and I stopped writing poetry
after graduating from that college on the Hudson,
though ten years later I started again and I haven't
stopped yet. Mark Anderson liked John Crowe Ransom
and Robert Penn Warren and Waylon Jennings.
Today he teaches English in a high school
in West Virginia. I liked e.e. cummings and May Swenson
and Paul Simon. Today I work as a sign language interpreter
in Boston, Massachusetts. We both liked Donald Justice
who lived and wrote and taught in Florida. I will die
in Florida, Mark Anderson will die in West Virginia,
Robert Kelly would have died a long time ago
if he hadn't lost the weight. Elizabeth Bishop
was an only child, like me, and published sparingly. John Ashbery
replaced Kelly as the resident poet at that college on the Hudson,
but that was a long time after I'd moved to Boston
and signed up for that first sign language class. Ashbery died
in New York at 90. I never cared for Ashbery
and I never cared for New York, though I grew up in New Jersey
just a stone's throw from the City. *A stone's throw*
in sign language is the thumb and forefinger

grazing the tip of the nose in a downward motion. I will die
in Florida because I married my sign language teacher
who was Deaf, and it didn't work out, so I married another
Deaf woman, which didn't work out either, so I married a third
Deaf woman and the third time's the charm—I never cared
for Florida but my third wife has convinced me
to retire in St. Augustine, where I'm sipping my tea
as I write this, a stone's throw from the Florida School for the Deaf
and the Blind. There are many live-oaks here in St. Augustine
uttering joyous leaves of dark green, the moss hanging down
from the branches, like in that Whitman poem
about a live-oak growing in Louisiana all alone. I will die alone
in Florida because we all die alone, perhaps remembering a poem
by Donald Justice, whose poems were short and memorable—
most of them fit on a single page—and whose output was small,
and who was an only child, like me, only in Miami.

The Idiot

This dusty old Dostoevsky novel—
one of the great books I never read
but lugged around with the other great
unread books as I moved from house to house

to this house finally, where I'll probably
die before I get around to reading this book,
old and moldering as it is, and I am. And I am
such an idiot, I think to myself, it's time
I threw out this book.

They called me Dostoevsky when I was a kid
because it kind of sounded like Hostovsky—
at least the tail end of it did—
and because I told them, "One day
I will be a famous writer, mark my words."
What an idiot!

I've been calling myself an idiot
a lot lately. Too much, probably. I'm not very
nice to me. If somebody else kept calling me an idiot,
I'd walk right up to him, my face in his face,
and ask him what his problem was—

What's your problem? I ask myself.
Yeah you. Yeah that word you keep calling me—
Do you want to make something out of it?

Dostoevsky was bellicose and testy.
He hired a stenographer, Anna Snitkina,
to help him write *The Idiot*
and *The Gambler.* He tested her dictation
by deliberately speaking so fast she couldn't keep up.

Then he married her. Then he gambled away
all their money. Then she took over
their finances and his publishing negotiations
and saved the day. He was a literary genius
and an idiot. She loved him anyway.
End of story.

"Life Is Sacred"

Yeah but
how do you know
it's so wonderful
not being dead yet?
I mean death is a wonder,
there's no getting around it.
Everyone wonders
where the dead have gone.
There are theories of course.
Theories of God, theories of heaven.
And science claims to know,
but science has made a bigger mess
of the world than God did,
if God did make the world,
which science says He didn't.
Between you and me,
I think we're all asleep in heaven
dreaming the world.
Life is but a dream,
like in that song about rowing
a boat. The one we sang in kindergarten.
It was a round, remember?
Different people coming in
and going out at different times.
And it went on that way
for some time until it all ended.
And then no one was singing.
Which felt a little sad but the silence
that hung in the air afterwards
was full of smiles.

O'Clock

The kitchen table was round.
The father sat at 9 o'clock
nearest the back door, the mother
at 3 o'clock nearest the stove,
the son at 6 o'clock across from the window
at 12. They weren't exactly assigned seats
like in school, where you looked out a window
at the trees across the street and wished
you were out there among them. But that was how
it ended up. When the father died
the son took his place at 9 o'clock
across from the mother, who remained
at 3 o'clock for five more years until
the son turned 18 and slipped out the back
door. Then she was all alone at the table
and we don't know where she sat.
And it's too late now to ask her.
Maybe she moved into the den
and ate in front of the television, which
had been verboten for a whole round-
table era. But more likely she remained
at 3 o'clock at that table in that kitchen
in that house where time passed heavily
like a bowl of peas being passed around
from mother to father to son,
who kept pushing them around on his plate
with his fork, for a whole only childhood,
trying to make them disappear.

My Favorite Part of the Vacation

was the movie on the flight home—
because the movie
moved me. Especially
that scene where the old man with no legs
was begging in the train station,
and the young thug accosted him with a knife,
and asked him why he didn't just
kill himself. I don't like going to places on vacation
where the people sit around all day getting tan
while certain other people, who are usually a darker, more
    beautiful hue
than the people on vacation could hope to achieve
in a lifetime, serve them. The old man
was trembling now, fearful for his life.
And he half-whispered, half-gasped:
"Because I still like to sit in the sun sometimes
and feel the sun on my face." And his face
was a beautiful walnut. And the young thug's face
was a beautiful walnut, too. And all of a sudden
I felt the hot tears on my face at 50 thousand feet
in the air-conditioned cabin. And it felt
good to finally feel something.
Because I'd spent all week on vacation
sitting at the pool and sitting on the beach
and eating out in restaurants every day
and feeling full and feeling useless and feeling
like nothing I was doing or feeling was feeding
that part of me that most needs feeding, which is exactly
what I tried explaining to you when in the middle
of the beef bourguignon and free cocktails in first class
you turned to tell me how wonderful it all was
and found me weeping silently over my tray table.

Found Poem

August
Seniors
Half-price

says the McDonald's sign
all of August.

I can't resist:
"I, an august senior,
will gladly pay you Tuesday

for a hamburger today,"
I say to the pimpled associate

behind the counter
just to see his unibrow
knit.

Priceless.

Bazooka

My father was older than all of the other fathers
and sick with colon cancer
in that room at the end of the hall
the one he'd moved into
to be alone
because of the pain
that was his alone
and because of the smell
coming from his room
and also faintly in the hall
where the little green
army men were killing each other off
with yelps and groans
and sounds of artillery fire
emanating from my lips and teeth and tongue

and when he came out
to go to the bathroom
he yelled at me for being in the way
and for being a little kid
playing on the floor outside his room
and making all that noise

so I aimed a green
plastic man with a bazooka
in his direction
as he padded slowly past me
in his gray pajamas
and old ratty bathrobe
with the belt trailing on the floor
and the smell of death in the air

and silently took him out

for which I felt so guilty
that I couldn't tell anyone
a few weeks later when he died
that I was the one
who killed him

Stealing Home

Down at the schoolyard Billy Schachtel was at bat. Richard Cohen was on first, Jon Winkelried on second. *Schachtel* means *box* in German. Little box. A pack of cigarettes is a *Zigarettenschachtel*. But none of us knew that. Because we didn't speak German. And we didn't smoke cigarettes. We were little. We were only in fourth grade. *Shtetl* means *little town* in Yiddish, a little town of Ashkenazi Jews in Eastern Europe before the Holocaust. But this was after the Holocaust, about twenty years after, at the bottom of the 9th in the schoolyard of South Mountain Elementary School in a mostly Jewish neighborhood in Millburn, New Jersey, in the United States of America, where Jews played baseball. Jews on *shtetls* in Eastern Europe didn't play baseball. And they never won. In fact, they usually got slaughtered. Schachtel swung and missed. We pronounced it Shack-TELL. Billy Shack-TELL. Not unlike William Tell, the Swiss folk hero and contemporary of Arnold von Winkelried, who threw himself on a Hapsburg spear in the Battle of Sempach, creating an opening for the Swiss Confederacy to rush in behind him and win the day. Winkelried was about to steal third. Cohen was on first, and maybe because the Cohanim were the Jewish priestly class, the judges, descendants of Aaron, brother of Moses, tribe of Levi, Cohen was able to judge that Winkelried was about to steal third. So he got ready to steal second. Which is called a *double steal* in baseball. With a judicious eye, Schachtel let the next pitch go by. Spoiler alert: Winkelried stole third, went on to steal home, and on to graduate from U. Chicago, get a job with Goldman Sachs, to work his way up till he headed the Bonds Department and became richer than Croesus, legendary king of Lydia, a kingdom in ancient Anatolia. Coney got thrown out at second, which was a kind of sacrifice that allowed Winkelried to steal home, not unlike the sacrifice that Winkelried's namesake made at the Battle of Sempach in 1386. It was the winning run at the bottom of the 9th, so Shachtel never finished his turn at bat. Because we'd already won, unlike the other Jews, the Jews of history, who almost always lost, and never really had a home.

Longevity

For as long as I live
I will keep coming back here,
making the trip alone
because there's nothing to do here
and no one to see here
and nowhere that isn't
not here. Standing across the street
from the house I grew up in,
which is the house I couldn't wait to leave,
I stare a long time at the nothingness
that no one else can see. Only I
can see it. I, the famous discoverer
of my only childhood.
I, the fastest kid on my block
until someone else was faster.
And then there was some question
about whether I was second fastest
or third. Somehow I slipped
into obscurity and adulthood
and no one has heard of me now
in my sixties, limping around
my old stomping grounds, my gimpy
leg smarting. I can't stop staring
at the old house—with its new
owners, new vinyl siding, new
roof with those expensive
metal shingles. There is no question
it will outlive me. I, who was famously
fleet-footed and immortal
back in my pimples.

About the Author

Paul Hostovsky's poems appear and disappear simultaneously (ta-da!) and have recently been sighted in places where they pay you for your trouble with your own trouble doubled, and other people's troubles thrown in, which never seem to him as great as his troubles, though he tries not to compare. He has no life and spends it with his poems, trying to perfect their perfect disappearances, which is the title of his newest collection, which it appears you are holding in your hands.

His disappearing poems have won a Pushcart Prize, two Best of the Net Awards, the FutureCycle Poetry Book Prize, the Muriel Craft Bailey Award, and five chapbook contests from Grayson Books, Riverstone Press, Frank Cat Press, Split Oak Press, and Sport Literate. He has been featured on *Poetry Daily, Verse Daily, Your Daily Poem, The Writer's Almanac,* and the *Best American Poetry* blog. He makes his living in Boston as a sign language interpreter and braille instructor. *Perfect Disappearances* is his fourteenth full-length collection.

www.ingramcontent.com/pod-product-compliance
Lightning Source LLC
Chambersburg PA
CBHW031202160426
43193CB00008B/472